A Woman's Book of
Inspiration

A Woman's Book of
Inspiration

edited by
CAROL KELLY-GANGI

New York

FALL RIVER PRESS

New York

An Imprint of Sterling Publishing
387 Park Avenue South
New York, NY 10016

Compilation © 2014 Fall River Press

The quotes in this book have been drawn from many sources, and
are assumed to be accurate as quoted in their previously published forms.
Although every effort has been made to verify the quotes and their sources,
the Publisher cannot guarantee their perfect accuracy.

Cover design by Patrice Kaplan

ISBN 978-1-4351-4841-3

For information about custom editions, special sales, and premium
and corporate purchases, please contact Sterling Special Sales
at 800-805-5489 or specialsales@sterlingpublishing.com.

Manufactured in the United States of America

2 4 6 8 10 9 7 5 3 1

www.sterlingpublishing.com

Contents

*To my mother and my daughter with eternal love—
you both truly inspire me every day.*

Introduction

One is not born a woman: one becomes one.
— SIMONE DE BEAUVOIR

What does it mean to be a woman in today's world? Women are facing new and increasing challenges in every sphere of life, yet it is also evident that women have faced seemingly insurmountable challenges from the dawn of recorded history. What is undoubtedly true is that women persevere. *A Woman's Book of Inspiration* gathers hundreds of quotations from women throughout history in the hopes of offering some additional insight into women and their ideas, reflections, and musings on a broad spectrum of subjects.

There are universal themes that inevitably emerge: the limitless love of family and children; the enduring struggle for equality; the quest for knowledge; and the endless pursuit to balance the commitments of work and family. The selections themselves, however, are as singular as the women who voiced them.

Helen Keller extols the value of optimism in the face of life's adversities; Louisa May Alcott reflects on the role that work has played in her life; and Jane Austen and Virginia Woolf each express the meaning of true friendship. In other selections, Hillary Rodham Clinton explains the particular effect of war on women; Margaret Thatcher and

Sheryl Sandberg speak about women and power; Eleanor Roosevelt offers her insights into achieving peace in the world; and Diane Sawyer refutes the notion that aging and isolation go hand in hand.

Elsewhere, women reveal some of the profound joys and struggles experienced in their own lives. Harriet Tubman recalls the moment she knew she would die for her freedom. Amelia Earhart defends her need to explore in spite of the dangers. Ruth Bader Ginsberg offers a heartfelt tribute to her own mother. Meryl Streep shares insights into how motherhood has changed her. Katharine Hepburn and Bette Davis supply wry commentary on the age-old question of how women and men relate.

In a dialogue that moves through time and place, the contributors also exchange views on such subjects as the meaning of love, the value of education, the notion of beauty, the role of spirituality, the art of communication, and the price of success.

A collection that speaks to not only women but also the richness of the human experience, *A Woman's Book of Inspiration* is a testament to women everywhere, today and through history, who embody a spirit of strength, determination, nurturing, and hope that is all their own.

—Carol Kelly-Gangi, 2013

Love and Friendship

Not all of us can do great things. But we can do small things with great love.

—MOTHER TERESA

Where there is great love there are always miracles.

—WILLA CATHER

Love is a flower that grows in any soil, works its sweet miracles undaunted by autumn frost or winter snow, blooming fair and fragrant all the year, and blessing those who give and those who receive.

—LOUISA MAY ALCOTT

Love makes your soul crawl out from its hiding place.

—ZORA NEALE HURSTON

How do I love thee? Let me count the ways.
I love thee to the depth and breadth and height
My soul can reach.

—ELIZABETH BARRETT BROWNING

How helpless we are, like netted birds, when we are
caught by desire!

—BELVA PLAIN

It was enough just to sit there without words.

—LOUISE ERDRICH

The loss of young first love is so painful that it borders on
the ludicrous.

—MAYA ANGELOU

Love at first sight is easy to understand; it's when two people have been looking at each other for a lifetime that it becomes a miracle.

—AMY BLOOM

Love is not enough. It must be the foundation, the cornerstone, but not the complete structure. It is much too pliable, too yielding.

—BETTE DAVIS

How did a person survive without intimacy? Didn't you need at least one person in the world to know who you really were?

—JUDITH FREEMAN

If love does not know how to give and take without restrictions, it is not love, but a transaction.

—EMMA GOLDMAN

What I cannot love, I overlook.

—ANAÏS NIN

It's so clear that you have to cherish everyone. I think that's what I get from these older black women, that every soul is to be cherished, that every flower is to bloom.

—ALICE WALKER

Is there any stab as deep as wondering where and how much you failed those you loved?

—FLORIDA SCOTT-MAXWELL

The most vital right is the right to love and be loved.

—EMMA GOLDMAN

That Love is all there is,
Is all we know of Love.

—EMILY DICKINSON

Friendship is the finest balm for the pangs of despised love.

—JANE AUSTEN

Friendship with oneself is all important because without it one cannot be friends with anybody else in the world.

—ELEANOR ROOSEVELT

Each friend represents a world in us, a world possibly not born until they arrive, and it is only by this meeting that a new world is born.

—ANAÏS NIN

The growth of true friendship may be a lifelong affair.

—SARAH ORNE JEWETT

Some people go to priests; others to poetry; I to my friends.

—VIRGINIA WOOLF

Familiarity breeds content.

—ANNA QUINDLEN

There's a kind of emotional exploration you plumb with a friend that you don't really do with your family.

—BETTE MIDLER

Only solitary men know the full joys of friendship. Others have their family; but to a solitary and an exile his friends are everything.

—WILLA CATHER

Happiness and Fulfillment

There is only one happiness in life, to love and be loved.

—GEORGE SAND

There is only one happiness in life, to love and be loved.

Happiness is not a matter of events; it depends upon the tides of the mind.

—ALICE MEYNELL

I have learned from experience that the greater part of our happiness or misery depends on our dispositions and not on our circumstances.

—MARTHA WASHINGTON

Life appears to me to be too short to be spent in nursing animosity or registering wrong.

—CHARLOTTE BRONTË

It's only possible to live happily ever after on a day-to-day basis.

—MARGARET BONNANO

Happiness is not a goal; it is a by-product.

—ELEANOR ROOSEVELT

Happiness is good health and a bad memory.

—INGRID BERGMAN

When one door of happiness closes, another opens; but often we look so long at the closed door that we do not see the one which has been opened for us.

—HELEN KELLER

If only we'd stop trying to be happy we could have a pretty good time.

—EDITH WHARTON

One half of the world cannot understand the pleasures of the other.

—JANE AUSTEN

Laughter by definition is healthy.

—DORIS LESSING

Eden is that old-fashioned house
We dwell in every day
Without suspecting our abode
Until we drive away.

—EMILY DICKINSON

Happiness is a matter of one's most ordinary and everyday mode of consciousness being busy and lively and unconcerned with self.

—IRIS MURDOCH

It is not what we see and touch or that which others do for us which makes us happy; it is that which we think and feel and do, first for the other fellow and then for ourselves.

—HELEN KELLER

When so rich a harvest is before us, why do we not gather it? All is in our hands if we will but use it.

—ST. ELIZABETH ANN SETON

Why not seize the pleasure at once? How often is happiness destroyed by preparation, foolish preparation!

—JANE AUSTEN

Everyone has inside of her a piece of good news. The good news is that you don't know how great you can be! How much you can love! What you can accomplish! And what your potential is!

—ANNE FRANK

Everything has its wonders, even darkness and silence, and I learn whatever state I may be in, therein to be content.

—HELEN KELLER

There are two ways of spreading light: to be the candle or the mirror that reflects it.

—EDITH WHARTON

What a wonderful life I've had! I only wish I'd realized it sooner.

—COLETTE

Marriage, Children, and Family

Happiness in marriage is entirely a matter of chance.

—JANE AUSTEN

The first great step is to like yourself enough to pick someone who likes you, too.

—JANE O'REILLY

That quiet mutual gaze of a trusting husband and wife is like the first moment of rest or refuge from a great weariness or a great danger.

—GEORGE ELIOT

Domestic peace! best joy of earth.
When shall we all thy value learn?

—ANNE BRONTË

Wasn't marriage, like life, unstimulating and unprofitable
and somewhat empty when too well ordered and protected
and guarded? Wasn't it finer, more splendid, more
nourishing, when it was, like life itself, a mixture of the
sordid and the magnificent; of mud and stars; of earth
and flowers; of love and hate and laughter and tears and
ugliness and beauty and hurt?

—EDNA FERBER

If you want to sacrifice the admiration of many men for
the criticism of one, go ahead, get married.

—KATHARINE HEPBURN

Why does a woman work ten years to change a man's habits
and then complain that he's not the man she married?

—BARBRA STREISAND

Once a woman has forgiven her man, she must not reheat his sins for breakfast.

—MARLENE DIETRICH

One of the trials of woman-kind is the fear of being an old maid. To escape this dreadful doom, young girls rush into matrimony with a recklessness which astonishes the beholder; never pausing to remember that the loss of liberty, happiness, and self-respect is poorly repaid by the barren honor of being called "Mrs." Instead of "Miss."

—LOUISA MAY ALCOTT

Bringing a child into the world is the greatest act of hope there is.

—LOUISE HART

Scratch a lover, and find a foe.

—DOROTHY PARKER

When a marriage ends, who is left to understand it?

—JOYCE CAROL OATES

A successful marriage requires falling in love many times, always with the same person.

—MIGNON MCLAUGHLIN

Making the decision to have a child—it's momentous. It is to decide forever to have your heart go walking around outside your body.

—ELIZABETH STONE

I do not consider divorce an evil by any means. It is just as much a refuge for women married to brutal men as Canada was to the slaves of brutal masters.

—SUSAN B. ANTHONY

Why had no one told me that my body would become a battlefield, a sacrifice, a test? Why did I not know that birth is the pinnacle where women discover the courage to become mothers?

—ANITA DIAMANT

Though motherhood is the most important of all professions—requiring more knowledge than any other department in human affairs—there was no attention given to preparation for this office.

—ELIZABETH CADY STANTON

A mother's love for her child is like nothing else in the world. It knows no law, no pity, it dares all things and crushes down remorselessly all that stands in its path.

—AGATHA CHRISTIE

Motherhood has a very humanizing effect. Everything gets reduced to essentials.

—MERYL STREEP

Even when you plan to have a family, you never know who the person is going to be that you decide to become a parent to. We're accidentally born to our own parents.

—LOUISE ERDRICH

Love and respect are the most important aspects of parenting, and of all relationships.

—JODIE FOSTER

You really do need a parent who's willing to set themselves aside, and their own hopes and dreams. If your child marches to a different beat, a different drummer, you might just have to go along with that music. Help them achieve what's important to them.

—SONIA SOTOMAYOR

Children require guidance and sympathy far more than instruction.

—ANNE SULLIVAN

Mummy herself has told us that she looked upon us more as her friends than her daughters. Now that is all very fine, but still, a friend can't take a mother's place.

—ANNE FRANK

If you bungle raising your children, I don't think whatever else you do well matters very much.

—JACQUELINE KENNEDY ONASSIS

I have a last thank-you. It is to my mother, Celia Amster Bader, the bravest and strongest person I have known, who was taken from me much too soon. I pray that I may be all that she would have been had she lived in an age when women could aspire and achieve and daughters are cherished as much as sons.

—RUTH BADER GINSBURG, on accepting her nomination to the U.S. Supreme Court, June 14, 1993

No matter how old a mother is, she watches her middle-aged children for signs of improvement.

—FLORIDA SCOTT-MAXWELL

By and large, mothers and housewives are the only workers who do not have regular time off. They are the great vacationless class.

—ANNE MORROW LINDBERGH

Being a mom has made me so tired. And so happy.

—TINA FEY

When men reach their sixties and retire, they go to pieces. Women go right on cooking.

—GAIL SHEEHY

Sister is probably the most competitive relationship within the family, but once the sisters are grown, it becomes the strongest relationship.

—MARGARET MEAD

I think a dysfunctional family is any family with more than one person in it.

—MARY KARR

Family life! The United Nations is child's play compared to the tugs and splits and need to understand and forgive in any family.

—MAY SARTON

One of the oldest human needs is having someone to wonder where you are when you don't come home at night.

—MARGARET MEAD

We are linked by blood, and blood is memory without language.

—JOYCE CAROL OATES

Life's Obstacles

I was taught that the way of progress is neither swift
nor easy.

—Marie Curie

We could never learn to be brave and patient, if there were
only joy in the world.

—Helen Keller

When you get into a tight place and it seems you can't go
on, hold on, for that's just the place and the time that the
tide will turn.

—Harriet Beecher Stowe

If you have made mistakes, even serious ones, there is always another chance for you. What we call failure is not the falling down, but the staying down.

—MARY PICKFORD

It is impossible to live without failing at something, unless you live so cautiously that you might as well not have lived at all—in which case, you fail by default.

—J. K. ROWLING

There are no mistakes, no coincidences. All events are blessings given to us to learn from.

—ELISABETH KÜBLER-ROSS

Please know that I am aware of the hazards. I want to do it because I want to do it. Women must try to do things as men have tried. When they fail, their failure must be but a challenge to others.

—AMELIA EARHART

I didn't have anybody, really, no foundation in life, so I had to make my own way. Always, from the start. I had to go out in the world and become strong, to discover my mission in life.

—TINA TURNER

A depressing and difficult passage has prefaced every new page I have turned in life.

—CHARLOTTE BRONTË

Illness is the night-side of life, a more onerous citizenship. Everyone who is born holds dual citizenship, in the kingdom of the well and in the kingdom of the sick.

—SUSAN SONTAG

I did not lose myself all at once. I rubbed out my face over the years washing away my pain, the same way carvings on stone are worn down by water.

—AMY TAN

I would like to learn, or remember, how to live.

—ANNIE DILLARD

Showing up for life. Being blessed with the rebirth that recovery brings.

One day at a time.

—BETTY FORD

A woman is like a tea bag. You never know how strong she is until she gets into hot water.

—ELEANOR ROOSEVELT

Great events make me quiet and calm; it is only trifles that irritate my nerves.

—QUEEN VICTORIA

We never know how high we are
'Til we are called to rise;
And then, if we are true to plan,
Our statures touch the skies.

—EMILY DICKINSON

I like living. I have sometimes been wildly, despairingly, acutely miserable, racked with sorrow, but through it all I still know quite certainly that just to be alive is a grand thing.

—AGATHA CHRISTIE

Education and Knowledge

My grandfather went to school for one day: to tell the teacher he wouldn't be back. Yet all of his life he read greedily, as did his uneducated friends.

—Toni Morrison

Home is a child's first and most important classroom.

—Hillary Rodham Clinton

Parents have become so convinced that educators know what is best for children that they forget that they themselves are really experts.

—Marian Wright Edelman

Anybody who has survived his childhood has enough information about life to last him the rest of his days.

—FLANNERY O'CONNOR

Part of teaching is helping students learn how to tolerate ambiguity, consider possibilities, and ask questions that are unanswerable.

—SARA LAWRENCE-LIGHTFOOT

Schooling is what happens inside the walls of the school, some of which is educational. Education happens everywhere, and it happens from the moment a child is born—and some people say before—until a child dies.

—SARA LAWRENCE-LIGHTFOOT

Sit down and read. Educate yourself for the coming conflicts.

—MOTHER JONES

The solution to my life occurred to me one evening while I was ironing a shirt.

—ALICE MUNRO

I'm going to college. I don't care if it ruins my career. I'd rather be smart than a movie star.

—NATALIE PORTMAN

The first problem for all of us, men and women, is not to learn, but to unlearn.

—GLORIA STEINEM

Prejudices, it is well known, are most difficult to eradicate from the heart whose soil has never been loosened or fertilized by education; they grow there, firm as weeds among rocks.

—CHARLOTTE BRONTË

The best-educated human being is the one who understands most about the life in which he is placed.

—HELEN KELLER

Think wrongly, if you please, but in all cases think for yourself.

—DORIS LESSING

Trust your hunches. They're usually based on facts filed away just below the conscious level.

—JOYCE BROTHERS

Every truth we see is one to give to the world, not to keep to ourselves alone.

—ELIZABETH CADY STANTON

If you have knowledge, let others light their candles at it.

—MARGARET FULLER

Freedom, Equality, and Justice

Those men and women are fortunate who are born at a time when a great struggle for human freedom is in progress.

—EMMELINE PANKHURST

None who have always been free can understand the terrible fascinating power of the hope of freedom to those who are not free.

—PEARL S. BUCK

I had reasoned this out in my mind, there were two things I had a right to: liberty and death. If I could not have one, I would have the other, for no man should take me alive.

—HARRIET TUBMAN

Freedom is fragile and must be protected. To sacrifice it, even as a temporary measure, is to betray it.

—GERMAINE GREER

Struggle is a never-ending process. Freedom is never really won; you earn it and win it in every generation.

—CORETTA SCOTT KING

We have only one real shot at liberation, and that is to emancipate ourselves from within.

—COLETTE DOWLING

Do not put such unlimited power into the hands of the Husbands. Remember, all Men would be tyrants if they could. If particular care and attention is not paid to the Ladies, we are determined to foment a Rebellion, and will not hold ourselves bound by any Laws in which we have no voice, or Representation.

—ABIGAIL ADAMS, letter to her husband, John, March 31, 1776

The day will come when man will recognize woman as his peer, not only at the fireside, but in councils of the nation. Then, and not until then, will there be the perfect comradeship, the ideal union between the sexes that shall result in the highest development of the race.

—SUSAN B. ANTHONY

I have ploughed, and planted, and gathered into barns, and no man could head me! And ain't I a woman? I could work as much and eat as much as a man—when I could get it—and bear the lash as well! And ain't I a woman?

—SOJOURNER TRUTH

I declare to you that woman must not depend upon the protection of man, but must be taught to protect herself, and there I take my stand.

—SUSAN B. ANTHONY

I am glad to see that men are getting their rights, but I want women to get theirs, and while the water is stirring I will step into the pool.

—Sojourner Truth

If society will not admit of woman's free development, then society must be remodeled.

—Elizabeth Blackwell

There is no female mind. The brain is not an organ of sex. Might as well speak of a female liver.

—Charlotte Perkins Gilman

I am neither a man nor a woman but an author.

—Charlotte Brontë

You have to be taught to be second class; you're not born that way.

—Lena Horne

If we are to achieve a richer culture, rich in contrasting values, we must recognize the whole gamut of human potentialities, and so weave a less arbitrary social fabric, one in which each diverse human gift will find a fitting place.

—MARGARET MEAD

No one can make you feel inferior without your consent.

—ELEANOR ROOSEVELT

I had felt for a long time, that if I was ever told to get up so a white person could sit, that I would refuse to do so.

—ROSA PARKS

I've run into more discrimination as a woman than as an Indian.

—WILMA PEARL MANKILLER

Of my two "handicaps," being female put many more obstacles in my path than being black.

—Shirley Chisholm

The time is at hand when the voices of the feminine mystique can no longer drown out the inner voice that is driving women on to become complete.

—Betty Friedan

"I hate discussions of feminism that end up with who does the dishes," she said. So do I. But at the end, there are always the damned dishes.

—Marilyn French

Some of us are becoming the men we wanted to marry.

—Gloria Steinem

Many of us are living out the unlived lives of our mothers, because they were not able to become the unique people they were born to be.

—Gloria Steinem

I am a candidate for the Presidency of the United States. I make that statement proudly, in the full knowledge that, as a black person and as a female person, I do not have a chance of actually gaining that office in this election year.

—Shirley Chisholm

We've chosen the path to equality; don't let them turn us around.

—Geraldine A. Ferraro

I especially treasure the young women who say that my example has inspired them to raise their sights so that they now feel that serving as secretary of state or in even higher office is a realistic goal.

—Madeleine Albright

A little girl grows up in Jim Crow Birmingham, and she becomes the secretary of state.

—CONDOLEEZZA RICE

Somewhere out in this audience may even be someone who will one day follow in my footsteps, and preside over the White House as the President's spouse. I wish him well!

—BARBARA BUSH

We are in the midst of a violent backlash against feminism.

—NAOMI WOLF

Real change will come when powerful women are less of an exception. It is easy to dislike senior women because there are so few.

—SHERYL SANDBERG

My address is like my shoes. It travels with me. I abide where there is a fight against wrong.

—MOTHER JONES

Social change rarely comes about through the efforts of the disenfranchised. The middle class creates social revolutions. When a group of people are disproportionately concerned with daily survival, it's not likely that they have the resources to go to Washington and march.

—FAYE WATTLETON

For all the injustices in our past and our present, we have to believe that in the free exchange of ideas, justice will prevail over injustice, tolerance over intolerance, and progress over reaction.

—HILLARY RODHAM CLINTON

Politics, War, and Peace

There is no hope even that woman, with her right to vote, will ever purify politics.

—Emma Goldman

Truthfulness has never been counted among the political virtues, and lies have always been regarded as justifiable tools in political dealings.

—Hannah Arendt

If American politics are too dirty for women to take part in, there's something wrong with American politics.

—Edna Ferber

You can't have a Congress that responds to the needs of the workingman when there are practically no people here who represent him. And you're not going to have a society that understands its humanity if you don't have more women in government.

—BELLA ABZUG

If you want to push something in politics you're accused of being aggressive, and that's not supposed to be a good thing for a woman. If you get upset and show it, you're accused of being emotional.

—MARY HARNEY

The first woman President will have to show that she has all of the marbles required to run the government on her own.

—DIANNE FEINSTEIN

We have made tremendous strides since 1920. Women have a stronger voice in our communities and in our workplace. I am proud to serve as one of the 14 women, Republican and Democrat, in the United States Senate, and now we have 62 women in the House of Representatives. We have made progress, but much more needs to be done.

—BARBARA BOXER, in a letter on the Anniversary of the Ratification of the 19th Amendment, August 18, 2003

The politicians were talking themselves red, white, and blue in the face.

—CLARE BOOTHE LUCE

The problem is, of course, that these interest groups are all asking for changes, but their enthusiasm for change rapidly disappears when it affects the core of their own interests.

—ANGELA MERKEL

I always cheer up immensely if an attack is particularly wounding because I think, well, if they attack one personally, it means they have not a single political argument left.

—MARGARET THATCHER

I'm also very proud to be a liberal. Why is that so terrible these days? The liberals were liberating. They fought slavery, fought for women to have the right to vote . . . fought to end segregation, fought to end apartheid. Thanks to the liberals, we have Social Security, public education, consumer and environmental protection, Medicare, Medicaid, the minimum-wage law, unemployment compensation. Liberals put an end to child labor. They even gave us the five-day work week. What's to be ashamed of?

—BARBRA STREISAND

The first Republican I knew was my father and he is still the Republican I most admire. He joined our party because the Democrats in Jim Crow Alabama of 1952 would not register him to vote. The Republicans did. My father has never forgotten that day, and neither have I.

— CONDOLEEZZA RICE

War is the unfolding of miscalculations.

— BARBARA TUCHMAN

I stand at the altar of the murdered men, and while I live, I fight their cause.

— FLORENCE NIGHTINGALE

You can no more win a war than you can win an earthquake.

— JEANETTE RANKIN

Women have always been the primary victims of war. Women lose their husbands, their fathers, their sons in combat.

—HILLARY RODHAM CLINTON

We've been a country that's been fortunate to be protected by two oceans, to not have serious attacks on our territory for most of our history. And we were unfortunately reminded in a very devastating way of our vulnerability.

—CONDOLEEZZA RICE

A leader who doesn't hesitate before he sends his nation into battle is not fit to be a leader.

—GOLDA MEIR

That is what leadership is all about: staking your ground ahead of where opinion is and convincing people, not simply following the popular opinion of the moment.

—DORIS KEARNS GOODWIN

In the future, there will be no female leaders. There will just be leaders.

—SHERYL SANDBERG

The only alternative to war is peace and the only road to peace is negotiations.

—GOLDA MEIR

For it isn't enough to talk about peace. One must believe in it. And it isn't enough to believe in it. One must work at it.

—ELEANOR ROOSEVELT

I can promise you that women working together—linked, informed, and educated—can bring peace and prosperity to this forsaken planet.

—ISABEL ALLENDE

Every act of love is a work of peace, no matter how small.

—MOTHER TERESA

Work, Success, and Fame

Across the curve of the earth, there are women getting up before dawn, in the blackness before the point of light, in the twilight before sunrise; there are women rising earlier than men and children to break the ice, to start the stove, to put up the pap, the coffee, the rice, to iron the pants, to braid the hair, to pull the day's water up from the well, to boil water for tea, to wash the children for school, to pull the vegetables and start the walk to market, to run to catch the bus for the work that is paid. I don't know when most women sleep.

—ADRIENNE RICH

God gives talent. Work transforms talent into genius.

—ANNA PAVLOVA

When I see the elaborate study and ingenuity displayed by women in the pursuit of trifles, I feel no doubt of their capacity for the most herculean undertakings.

—JULIA WARD HOWE

Find something you're passionate about and keep tremendously interested in it.

—JULIA CHILD

Never work just for money or for power. They won't save your soul or help you sleep at night.

—MARIAN WRIGHT EDELMAN

A woman will always have to be better than a man in any job she undertakes.

—ELEANOR ROOSEVELT

What is sad for women of my generation is that they weren't supposed to work if they had families. What were they going to do when the children are grown—watch the raindrops coming down the windowpane?

—Jacqueline Kennedy Onassis

But the problem is that when I go around and speak on campuses, I still don't get young men standing up and saying, "How can I combine career and family?"

—Gloria Steinem

At work, you think of the children you have left at home. At home, you think of the work you've left unfinished. Such a struggle is unleashed within yourself. Your heart is rent.

—Golda Meir

You tell me who has to leave the office when the kid bumps his head or slips on a milk carton.

—Wendy Wasserstein

Careers are a jungle gym, not a ladder.

—SHERYL SANDBERG

I don't believe in careers. I believe in work.

—DEBRA WINGER

I believe in hard work. It keeps the wrinkles out of the mind and the spirit. It helps to keep a woman young.

—HELENA RUBINSTEIN

Opportunities are usually disguised as hard work, so most people don't recognize them.

—ANN LANDERS

Laziness may appear attractive, but work gives satisfaction.

—ANNE FRANK

When you cease to make a contribution, you begin to die.

—ELEANOR ROOSEVELT

I've never sought success in order to get fame and money; it's the talent and the passion that count in success.

—INGRID BERGMAN

Success can make you go one of two ways. It can make you a prima donna, or it can smooth the edges, take away the insecurities, let the nice things come out.

—BARBARA WALTERS

I've always believed that one woman's success can only help another woman's success.

—GLORIA VANDERBILT

It is better to be young in your failures than old in your successes.

—FLANNERY O'CONNOR

The penalty of success is to be bored by people who used to snub you.

—LADY NANCY ASTOR

The secret of joy in work is contained in one word— excellence. To know how to do something well is to enjoy it.

—PEARL S. BUCK

When you perform . . . you are out of yourself—larger and more potent, more beautiful. You are for minutes heroic. This is power. This is glory on earth. And it is yours, nightly.

—AGNES DE MILLE

When I'm performing, I'm not afraid of anything or anybody. But when I'm just me, I have this fright of being a disappointment to the people.

—BARBRA STREISAND

I restore myself when I'm alone. A career is born in public—talent in privacy.

—MARILYN MONROE

You really can't function as a celebrity. Entertainers are celebrities. I'm an architect. I'm an artist. I make things.

—MAYA LIN

Fame lost its appeal for me when I went into a public restroom and an autograph seeker handed me a pen and paper under the stall door.

—MARLO THOMAS

The best fame is a writer's fame: it's enough to get a table at a good restaurant, but not enough that you get interrupted when you eat.

—FRAN LEBOWITZ

I want to be known as an actress. I'm not royalty.

—Elizabeth Taylor

Celebrity is the religion of our time.

—Maureen Dowd

If you survive long enough, you're revered—rather like an old building.

—Katharine Hepburn

I am independent! I can live alone and I love to work.

—Mary Cassatt

Work is and always has been my salvation and I thank the Lord for it.

—Louisa May Alcott

Women and Beauty

Barefoot or first thing in the morning, I feel beautiful.
I didn't always feel that way, but I feel that way now.
When somebody loves you, and when you make
somebody else happy, when your presence seems to
make them happy, you suddenly feel like the most
beautiful person in the world.

— ANGELINA JOLIE

The girls who were unanimously considered beautiful
often rested on their beauty alone. I felt I had to do things,
to be intelligent and develop a personality in order to be
seen as attractive. By the time I realized maybe I wasn't
plain and might even possibly be pretty, I had already
trained myself to be a little more interesting and informed.

— DIANE VON FÜRSTENBERG

Any girl can be glamorous; all you have to do is stand still and look stupid.

—HEDY LAMARR

Brains are an asset—if you hide them.

—MAE WEST

The fact of the matter is that you can use your beauty and use your charm and be flirtatious, and you can get people interested in your beauty. But you cannot maintain that. In the end, talent is the only thing. My work is the only thing that's going to change any minds.

—MADONNA

Let me tell you something—being thought of as a beautiful woman has spared me nothing in life. No heartache, no trouble. Love has been difficult. Beauty is essentially meaningless and it is always transitory.

—HALLE BERRY

Character contributes to beauty. It fortifies a woman as her youth fades. A mode of conduct, a standard of courage, discipline, fortitude, and integrity can do a great deal to make a woman beautiful.

—JACQUELINE BISSET

The most difficult thing in the world is to start a career known only for your looks, and then to try to become a serious actress. No one will take you seriously once you are known as the pretty woman.

—PENÉLOPE CRUZ

Because too much of my life was spent waiting to be seen. Hoping to be seen, hoping to be picked. Once you realize that you aren't looked at that way anymore, other things start to happen and you have to depend on other things to get by.

—DIANE KEATON

Women have face-lifts in a society in which women without them appear to vanish from sight.

—NAOMI WOLF

There are some implausible standards out there. It's really sad when I spend time with girls who are 11 years old and think they're fat.

—JENNIFER CONNELLY

The psychic scars caused by believing you are ugly have a permanent mark on your personality.

—JOAN RIVERS

There's nothing moral about beauty.

—NADINE GORDIMER

I think your whole life shows in your face and you should be proud of that.

—LAUREN BACALL

Ava Gardner was the most beautiful woman in the world, and it's wonderful that she didn't cut up her face. She addressed aging by picking up her chin and receiving the light in a better way. And she looked like a woman. She never tried to look like a girl.

—SHARON STONE

The body is a sacred garment. It's your first and last garment; it is what you enter life in and what you depart life with, and it should be treated with honor.

—MARTHA GRAHAM

There should be more diversity. There are all different kinds of beauty in the world. I mean, why aren't mothers glorified? Instead, sex goddesses are glorified!

—JENNIFER CONNELLY

The Art of
Communication

The opposite of talking is not listening. The opposite of talking is waiting.

—Fran Lebowitz

When we speak we are afraid our words will not be heard or welcomed. But when we are silent, we are still afraid. So it is better to speak.

—Audre Lorde

Many times in life I've regretted the things I've said without thinking. But I've never regretted the things I said nearly as much as the words I left unspoken.

—Lisa Kleypas

We are stronger when we listen, and smarter when we share.

—RANIA AL ABDULLAH

Blessed is the man who, having nothing to say, abstains from giving us wordy evidence of the fact.

—GEORGE ELIOT

Tact is the art of making people feel at home when that's where you wish they were.

—ANN LANDERS

Good communication is as stimulating as black coffee, and just as hard to sleep after.

—ANNE MORROW LINDBERGH

Most conversations are simply monologues delivered in the presence of witnesses.

—MARGARET MILLAR

Polite conversation is rarely either.

—FRAN LEBOWITZ

Television has proved that people will look at anything rather than each other.

—ANN LANDERS

If you haven't got anything nice to say about anybody, come sit next to me.

—ALICE ROOSEVELT LONGWORTH

Everything we say signifies; everything counts, that we put out into the world. It impacts on kids, it impacts on the zeitgeist of the time.

—MERYL STREEP

I found I could say things with colors that I couldn't say in any other way—things that I had no words for.

—GEORGIA O'KEEFFE

The body says what words cannot.

—MARTHA GRAHAM

The ability of writers to imagine what is not the self, to familiarize the strange and mystify the familiar, is the test of their power.

—TONI MORRISON

To know how to say what others only know how to think is what makes men poets or sages; and to dare to say what others only dare to think makes men martyrs or reformers or both.

—ELIZABETH CHARLES

I think that education is power. I think that being able to communicate with people is power. One of my main goals on the planet is to encourage people to empower themselves.

—OPRAH WINFREY

Women and Men

In societies where men are truly confident of their own worth, women are not merely tolerated but valued.

—Aung San Suu Kyi

Men often say that women change their minds too much. I say they sometimes don't change them enough. I mean, changing their state of mind, their attitudes, their outlook, their expectations, their consciousness—most of all, about themselves and what is possible in their lives.

—Julia Alvarez

I've got a woman's ability to stick to a job and get on with it when everyone else walks off and leaves it.

—Margaret Thatcher

The economic dependence of women is perhaps the greatest injustice that has been done to us, and has worked the greatest injury to the race.

—NELLIE MCCLUNG

Have you any notion how many books are written about women in the course of one year? Have you any notion how many are written by men? Are you aware that you are, perhaps, the most discussed animal in the universe?

—VIRGINIA WOOLF

The especial genius of women I believe to be electrical in movement, intuitive in function, spiritual in tendency.

—MARGARET FULLER

Toughness doesn't have to come in a pinstripe suit.

—DIANNE FEINSTEIN

Among poor people, there's not any question about women being strong—even stronger than men—they work in the fields right along with the men. When your survival is at stake, you don't have these questions about yourself like middle-class women do.

—DOLORES HUERTA

Social science affirms that a woman's place in society marks the level of civilization.

—ELIZABETH CADY STANTON

Whether women are better than men I cannot say—but I can say they are certainly no worse.

—GOLDA MEIR

Men have had every advantage of us in telling their own story. Education has been theirs in so much higher a degree; the pen has been in their hands.

—JANE AUSTEN

Women are systematically degraded by receiving the trivial attentions which men think it manly to pay to the sex, when, in fact, men are insultingly supporting their own superiority.

—Mary Wollstonecraft

I'd much rather be a woman than a man. Women can cry, they can wear cute clothes, and they're the first to be rescued off sinking ships.

—Gilda Radner

Sometimes I wonder if men and women really suit each other. Perhaps they should live next door and just visit now and then.

—Katharine Hepburn

If men ever discovered how tough women actually are, they would be scared to death.

—Edna Ferber

I have the heart of a man, not a woman, and I am not afraid of anything.

—ELIZABETH I

I am a woman meant for a man, but I never found a man who could compete.

—BETTE DAVIS

Women who set a low value on themselves make life hard for all women.

—NELLIE MCCLUNG

What is most beautiful in virile men is something feminine; what is most beautiful in feminine women is something masculine.

—SUSAN SONTAG

Life's Pleasures

I'm afraid I'm an incorrigible life-lover, life-wonderer, and adventurer.

—EDITH WHARTON

———

Those who contemplate the beauty of the earth find reserves of strength that will endure as long as life lasts.

—RACHEL CARSON

———

The best remedy for those who are afraid, lonely, or unhappy is to go outside, somewhere where they can be quiet, alone with the heavens, nature, and God. Because only then does one feel that all is as it should be and that God wishes to see people happy, amidst the simple beauty of nature.

—ANNE FRANK

———

Flowers are heaven's masterpiece.

—DOROTHY PARKER

Any adult who spends even fifteen minutes with a child outdoors finds himself drawn back to his own childhood, like Alice falling down the rabbit hole.

—SHARON MACLATCHIE

Animals are such agreeable friends—they ask no questions, they pass no criticisms.

—GEORGE ELIOT

I think I should have no other mortal wants, if I could always have plenty of music. It seems to infuse strength into my limbs, and ideas into my brain. Life seems to go on without effort, when I am filled with music.

—GEORGE ELIOT

A house is no home unless it contains food and fire for the mind as well as for the body.

—MARGARET FULLER

Just the knowledge that a good book is waiting one at the end of a long day makes that day happier.

—KATHLEEN NORRIS

Please, no matter how we advance technologically, please don't abandon the book. There is nothing in our material world more beautiful than the book.

—PATTI SMITH

God comes to us in theater in the way we communicate with each other, whether it be a symphony orchestra, or a wonderful ballet, or a beautiful painting, or a play. It's a way of expressing our humanity.

—JULIE HARRIS

Poetry, I have discovered, is always unexpected and always as faithful and honest as dreams.

—ALICE WALKER

In books I have traveled, not only to other worlds, but into my own.

—ANNA QUINDLEN

The dancer's body is simply the luminous manifestation of the soul.

—ISADORA DUNCAN

Somewhere behind the athlete you've become and the hours of practice and the coaches who have pushed you is a little girl who fell in love with the game and never looked back . . . play for her.

—MIA HAMM

To travel is worth any cost or sacrifice.

—ELIZABETH GILBERT

The game of baseball has always been linked in my mind with the mystic texture of childhood, with the sounds and smells of summer nights, and with the memories of my father.

—DORIS KEARNS GOODWIN

Shopping is a woman thing. It's a contact sport like football. Women enjoy the scrimmage, the noisy crowds, the danger of being trampled to death, and the ecstasy of the purchase.

—ERMA BOMBECK

Cooking is like love. It should be entered into with abandon or not at all.

—HARRIET VAN HORNE

I finally figured out the only reason to be alive is to enjoy it.

—RITA MAE BROWN

Spirituality

From the moment a soul has the grace to know God, she must seek.

—MOTHER TERESA

The essential thing to know about God is that God is Good. All the rest is secondary.

—SIMONE WEIL

It is this belief in a power larger than myself and other than myself which allows me to venture into the unknown and even the unknowable.

—MAYA ANGELOU

God has always been to me not so much like a father as like a dear and tender mother.

—HARRIET BEECHER STOWE

I believe that God is in me as the sun is in the color and fragrance of a flower—the Light in my darkness, the Voice in my silence.

—HELEN KELLER

For prayer is the language of the heart,—needing no measured voice, no spoken tone.

—GRACE AGUILAR

Prayer is not asking. Prayer is putting oneself in the hands of God, at his disposition, and listening to his voice in the depths of our hearts.

—MOTHER TERESA

Learn to get in touch with the silence within yourself and know that everything in this life has a purpose.

—ELISABETH KÜBLER-ROSS

Intuition is a spiritual faculty, and does not explain, but simply points the way.

—FLORENCE SCOVEL SHINN

Meditation is the ultimate mobile device; you can use it anywhere, anytime, unobtrusively.

—SHARON SALZBERG

If women were convinced that a day off or an hour of solitude was a reasonable ambition, they would find a way of attaining it. As it is, they feel so unjustified in their demand that they rarely make the attempt.

—ANNE MORROW LINDBERGH

Grace fills empty spaces, but it can only enter where there is a voice to receive it, and it is grace itself which makes this void.

—SIMONE WEIL

Beauty and grace are performed whether or not we sense them. The least we can do is try to be there.

—ANNIE DILLARD

One thing that I ask of you: Never be afraid of giving. There is a deep joy in giving, since what we receive is much more than what we give.

—MOTHER TERESA

If you're going to care about the fall of the sparrow you can't pick and choose who's going to be the sparrow. It's everybody.

—MADELEINE L'ENGLE

This world is not conclusion.
A sequel stands beyond—
Invisible, as music—
But positive, as sound.

—EMILY DICKINSON

I believe in the immortality of the soul because I have within me immortal longings.

—HELEN KELLER

Character, Morality, and Virtue

The real things haven't changed. It is still best to be honest and truthful; to make the most of what we have; to be happy with simple pleasures; and have courage when things go wrong.

—Laura Ingalls Wilder

Courage: the most important of all the virtues because without courage, you can't practice any other virtue consistently.

—Maya Angelou

Standing for right when it is unpopular is a true test of moral character.

—Margaret Chase Smith

Simple, genuine goodness is the best capital to found the business of this life upon. It lasts when fame and money fail, and is the only riches we can take out of this world with us.

—LOUISA MAY ALCOTT

Being considerate of others will take you and your children further in life than any college or professional degree.

—MARIAN WRIGHT EDELMAN

The real test of class is how you treat people who cannot possibly do you any good.

—ANN LANDERS

The one thing that doesn't abide by majority rule is a person's conscience.

—HARPER LEE

The act of acting morally is behaving *as if everything we do matters.*

—GLORIA STEINEM

As a family, we had a code, which was to do the right thing, do it the best we could, never complain and never take advantage.

—MARGARET TRUMAN

Parents can only give good advice or put them on the right paths, but the final forming of a person's character lies in their own hands.

—ANNE FRANK

Nothing comes of so many things, if you have patience.

—JOYCE CAROL OATES

Humility must always be doing its work like a bee making its honey in the hive: without humility all will be lost.

—ST. TERESA OF ÁVILA

The truth needs so little rehearsal.

—BARBARA KINGSOLVER

The liar leads an existence of unutterable loneliness.

—ADRIENNE RICH

When hope is taken away from the people, moral degeneration follows swiftly after.

—PEARL S. BUCK

Our deeds still travel with us from afar,
And what we have been makes us what we are.

—GEORGE ELIOT

Poverty and Riches

To live in poverty is to live with constant uncertainty, to accept galling indignities, and to expect harassment by the police, welfare officials, and employers, as well as by others who are poor and desperate.

—BARBARA EHRENREICH

Hungry people cannot be good at learning or producing anything, except perhaps violence.

—PEARL BAILEY

Poverty is not about color.

—QUEEN LATIFAH

Loneliness and the feeling of being unwanted is the most terrible poverty.

—MOTHER TERESA

Money helps, though not so much as you think when you don't have it.

—LOUISE ERDRICH

The greatest thing I ever was able to do was give a welfare check back.

—WHOOPI GOLDBERG

The only way not to think of money is to have a great deal of it.

—EDITH WHARTON

I've been rich and I've been poor; Believe me honey, rich is better.

—SOPHIE TUCKER

Economy was always "elegant," and money-spending always "vulgar" and ostentatious—a sort of sour-grapeism, which made us very peaceful and satisfied.

—ELIZABETH GASKELL

I don't know much about being a millionaire, but I'll bet I'd be darling at it.

—DOROTHY PARKER

Perhaps too much of everything is as bad as too little.

—EDNA FERBER

I'd rather have roses on my table than diamonds on my neck.

—EMMA GOLDMAN

I never hated a man enough to give him his diamonds back.

—ZSA ZSA GABOR

I don't want to make money. I just want to be wonderful.

—MARILYN MONROE

Until we end the masculinization of wealth, we will not end the feminization of poverty.

—GLORIA STEINEM

It is easy to be independent when you've got money. But to be independent when you haven't got a thing, that's the Lord's test.

—MAHALIA JACKSON

Yesterday, Today, and Tomorrow

One faces the future with one's past.

—PEARL S. BUCK

—

Anyone who limits her vision to memories of yesterday is already dead.

—LILY LANGTRY

—

History, despite its wrenching pain, cannot be unlived, but if faced with courage, need not be lived again.

—MAYA ANGELOU

—

We inhabit ourselves without valuing ourselves, unable to see that here, now, this very moment is sacred; but once it's gone—its value is incontestable.

—JOYCE CAROL OATES

It is terribly amusing how many different climates of feeling one can go through in a day.

—ANNE MORROW LINDBERGH

You had better live your best and act your best and think your best today; for today is the sure preparation for tomorrow and all the other tomorrows that follow.

—HARRIET MARTINEAU

Today the problem that has no name, is how to juggle work, love, home, and children.

—BETTY FRIEDAN

It's not perfect, but to me on balance Right Now is a lot better than the Good Old Days.

—MAEVE BINCHY

There are years that ask questions and years that answer.

—ZORA NEALE HURSTON

Old age is like a plane flying through a storm. Once you are aboard there is nothing you can do.

—GOLDA MEIR

The future depends entirely on what each of us does every day.

—GLORIA STEINEM

The future belongs to those who believe in the beauty of their dreams.

—ELEANOR ROOSEVELT

Women may be the one group that grows more radical with age.

—GLORIA STEINEM

You need only claim the events of your life to make yourself yours. When you truly possess all you have been and done, which may take some time, you are fierce with reality.

—FLORIDA SCOTT-MAXWELL

Surely the consolation prize of age is in finding out how few things are worth worrying over, and how many things that we once desired, we don't want anymore.

—DOROTHY DIX

One does not get better but different and older and that is always a pleasure.

—GERTRUDE STEIN

What I don't understand is this assumption that aging means isolation. There's just so much to do in the world— so many people who need an ally, so many children who need hugging. I refuse to believe being elderly and being lonely go hand in hand.

—Diane Sawyer

I have always felt that a woman had the right to treat the subject of her age with ambiguity until, perhaps, she passed into the realm of over ninety. Then it is better she be candid with herself and with the world.

—Helena Rubinstein

For years I wanted to be older, and now I am.

—Margaret Atwood

The years seem to rush by now, and I think of death as a fast-approaching end of a journey—double and treble reason for loving as well as working while it is day.

—George Eliot

Dying seems less sad than having lived too little.

—GLORIA STEINEM

You don't get to choose how you're going to die. Or when. You can decide how you're going to live now.

—JOAN BAEZ

At the end of your life you will never regret not having passed one more test, winning one more verdict, or not closing one more deal. You will regret time not spent with a husband, a child, a friend, or a parent.

—BARBARA BUSH

Wisdom and Inspiration

Figuring out who you are is the whole point of the human experience.

—ANNA QUINDLEN

Our deepest wishes are whispers of our authentic selves. We must learn to respect them. We must learn to listen.

—SARAH BAN BREATHNACH

One of the lessons that I grew up with was to always stay true to yourself and never let what somebody else says distract you from your goals. And so when I hear about negative and false attacks, I really don't invest any energy in them, because I know who I am.

—MICHELLE OBAMA

I think the key is for women not to set any limits.

—MARTINA NAVRATILOVA

I think when we experience emotion we should delve into it and live through it. We are always trying to shut off pain or control our happiness. Why? To live is to feel.

—GWYNETH PALTROW

I don't think of all the misery, but of the beauty that still remains.

—ANNE FRANK

Our way is not soft grass, it's a mountain path with lots of rocks. But it goes upwards, forward, toward the sun.

—RUTH WESTHEIMER

No pessimist ever discovered the secrets of the stars, or sailed to an uncharted land, or opened a new heaven to the human spirit.

—HELEN KELLER

If you can't change your fate, change your attitude.

—AMY TAN

Bloom where you are planted.

—MARY ENGELBREIT

You can't shake hands with a clenched fist.

—INDIRA GANDHI

What people in the world think of you is really none of your business.

—MARTHA GRAHAM

Being powerful is like being a lady. If you have to tell people you are, you aren't.

—MARGARET THATCHER

The most common way people give up their power is by thinking they don't have any.

—ALICE WALKER

I don't need a man to rectify my existence. The most profound relationship we'll ever have is the one with ourselves.

—SHIRLEY MACLAINE

Measure not the work until the day's out and the labor done.

—ELIZABETH BARRETT BROWNING

Surround yourself with only people who are going to lift you higher.

—OPRAH WINFREY

Women have to summon up courage to fulfill dormant dreams.

—ALICE WALKER

Imagine that we conjure up a world that is safe for mothers and daughters.

—LOUISE BERNIKOW

Luck is a matter of preparation meeting opportunity.

—OPRAH WINFREY

Follow what you are genuinely passionate about and let that guide you to your destination.

—DIANE SAWYER

Exhaust the little moment. Soon it dies.
And be it gash or gold it will not come
Again in this identical disguise.

—GWENDOLYN BROOKS

Cherish your solitude. Take trains by yourself to places you have never been. Sleep out alone under the stars. Learn how to drive a stick shift. Go so far away that you stop being afraid of not coming back. Say no when you don't want to do something. Say yes if your instincts are strong, even if everyone around you disagrees. Decide whether you want to be liked or admired. Decide if fitting in is more important than finding out what you're doing here. Believe in kissing.

—EVE ENSLER

Life was meant to be lived, and curiosity must be kept alive. One must never, for whatever reason, turn one's back on life.

—ELEANOR ROOSEVELT

Contributors

Bella Abzug (1920–1998) — American politician

Abigail Adams (1744–1818) — Writer and wife of John Adams, second U.S. President

Grace Aguilar (1816–1847) — English writer and theologian

Rania Al Abdullah (b. 1970) — Kuwait-born Queen of Jordan and wife of King Abullah II

Madeleine Albright (b. 1937) — Czech-born American public official and first woman to become the U.S. Secretary of State

Louisa May Alcott (1832–1888) — American novelist

Isabel Allende (b. 1942) — Chilean writer

Julia Alvarez (b. 1950) — American writer

Maya Angelou (b. 1928) — American writer and poet

Susan B. Anthony (1820–1906) — Pioneer in U.S. women's suffrage movement

Hannah Arendt (1906–1975) — German-born American political philosopher and writer

Lady Nancy Astor (1879–1964) — English Viscountess, first woman MP in the British House of Commons

Margaret Atwood (b. 1939) — Canadian writer and activist

Jane Austen (1775–1817) — English novelist

Lauren Bacall (b. 1924) — American actress and writer

Joan Baez (b. 1941) — American folksinger, songwriter, musician, and activist

Pearl Bailey (1918–1990) — American singer

Sarah Ban Breathnach (b. 1948) — English writer

Ingrid Bergman (1915–1982) — Swedish actress

Louise Berkinow (b. 1940) — American writer and activist

Halle Berry (b. 1966) — American actress and model

Maeve Binchy (1940–2012) — Irish writer

Jacqueline Bisset (b. 1944) — English actress

Elizabeth Blackwell (1821–1910) — American physician, first female medical doctor in the United States

Amy Bloom (b. 1953) — American writer

Erma Bombeck (1927–1996) — American humorist and writer

Margaret Bonnano (b. 1950) — American writer

Barbara Boxer (b. 1940) — American politician

Anne Brontë (1820–1849) — English novelist and poet

Charlotte Brontë (1816–1855) — English novelist and poet

Gwendolyn Brooks (1917–2000) — American poet

Joyce Brothers (1925–2013) — American psychologist and writer

Rita Mae Brown (b. 1944) — American writer and activist

Elizabeth Barrett Browning (1806–1861) — English poet

Pearl S. Buck (1892–1973) — American novelist

Barbara Bush (b. 1925) — Former First Lady of the United States and humanitarian

Rachel Carson (1907–1964) — American marine biologist, conservationist, and writer

Mary Cassatt (1844–1926) — American painter

Willa Cather (1873–1947) — American novelist, poet, journalist, and editor

Elizabeth Charles (1828–1896) — English writer

Julia Child (1912–2004) — American chef, writer, and television personality

Shirley Chisholm (1924–2005) — American politician, educator, and writer

Agatha Christie (1890–1976) — English writer

Hillary Rodham Clinton (b. 1947) — Former U.S. Secretary of State, and former First Lady of the United States

Colette (1873–1954) — French novelist and performer

Jennifer Connelly (b. 1970) — American actress

Penélope Cruz (b. 1974) — Spanish actress and model

Marie Curie (1867–1934) — French-Polish physicist and chemist

Bette Davis (1908–1989) — American actress

Simone de Beauvoir (1908–1986) — French novelist and activist

Agnes de Mille (1905–1993) — American choreographer, dancer, and writer

Anita Diamant (b. 1951) — American writer

Emily Dickinson (1830–1886) — American poet

Marlene Dietrich (1901–1992) — German-born actress and singer

Annie Dillard (b. 1945) — American writer and professor

Dorothy Dix (1861–1951) — American journalist

Maureen Dowd (b. 1952) — American journalist and writer

Colette Dowling (b. 1938) — American psychotherapist and writer

Isadora Duncan (1877–1927) — American dancer

Amelia Earhart (1897–1937?) — American aviator and writer

Marian Wright Edelman (b. 1939) — American children's rights activist

Barbara Ehrenreich (b. 1941) — American writer and activist

George Eliot (1819–1880) — English novelist

Elizabeth I (1533–1603) — British monarch

Mary Engelbreit (b. 1952) — American artist and illustrator

Eve Ensler (b. 1953) — American writer, performer, and activist

Louise Erdrich (b. 1954) — American writer

Dianne Feinstein (b. 1933) — American politician

Edna Ferber (1887–1968) — American novelist and playwright

Geraldine A. Ferraro (1935–2011) — American lawyer and politician

Tina Fey (b. 1970) — American actress, writer, comedian, and producer

Betty Ford (1918–2011) — Former First Lady of the United States, and co-founder of The Betty Ford Center

Jodie Foster (b. 1962) — American actress, director, and producer

Anne Frank (1929–1945) — German diarist

Judith Freeman (b. 1946) — American writer

Marilyn French (1929–2009) — American writer

Betty Friedan (1921–2006) — American writer and activist

Margaret Fuller (1810–1850) — American journalist and critic

Zsa Zsa Gabor (b. 1917) — Hungarian-born American actress and socialite

Elizabeth Gaskell (1810–1865) — English writer

Indira Gandhi (1917–1984) — Four-time Prime Minister of India who was assassinated in 1984

Elizabeth Gilbert (b. 1969) — American writer

Charlotte Perkins Gilman (1860–1935) — American writer and lecturer

Ruth Bader Ginsberg (b. 1933) — U.S. Supreme Court Justice

Whoopi Goldberg (b. 1955) — American actress, comedian, activist, writer, and talk-show host

Emma Goldman (1869–1940) — Russian-born American writer, anarchist, and activist

Doris Kearns Goodwin (b. 1943) — American biographer, historian, and political commentator

Nadine Gordimer (b. 1923) — South African writer and political activist

Martha Graham (1894–1991) — American dancer and choreographer

Germaine Greer (b. 1939) — Australian writer and activist

Mia Hamm (b. 1972) — American professional soccer player (retired) and writer

Mary Harney (b. 1953) — Irish politician

Julie Harris (1925–2013) — American actress

Louise Hart (b. 19??) — American psychologist, writer, and speaker

Katharine Hepburn (1907–2003) — American actress

Lena Horne (1917–2010) — American singer, actress, dancer, and activist

Julia Ward Howe (1819–1910) — American abolitionist, activist, and writer

Dolores Huerta (b. 1930) — American labor leader and activist

Zora Neale Hurston (1891–1960) — American writer, folklorist, and anthropologist

Mahalia Jackson (1911–1972) — American gospel singer

Sarah Orne Jewett (1849–1909) — American novelist and short-story writer

Angelina Jolie (b. 1975) — American actress, writer, director, and humanitarian

Mother Jones (1837–1930) — Irish-American labor organizer and humanitarian, a.k.a. Mary Harris Jones

Mary Karr (b. 1955) — American poet, writer, and professor

Diane Keaton (b. 1946) — American actress, director, producer, and screenwriter

Helen Keller (1880–1968) — American writer, activist, and educator

Coretta Scott King (1927–2006) — American activist and wife of Dr. Martin Luther King, Jr.

Barbara Kingsolver (b. 1955) — American writer

Lisa Kleypas (b. 1964) — American writer

Elisabeth Kübler-Ross (1926–2004) — Swiss-American psychiatrist and writer

Hedy Lamarr (1913–2000) — Austro-American actress and inventor

Ann Landers (1918–2002) — American advice columnist and talk-show host

Lily Langtry (1853–1929) — English actress

Queen Latifah (b. 1970) — American singer/songwriter, rap artist, model, and actress

Sara Lawrence-Lightfoot (b. 1944) — American sociologist

Fran Lebowitz (b. 1950) — American writer and social critic

Harper Lee (b. 1926) — American writer

Madeleine L'Engle (1918–2007) — American writer

Doris Lessing (1919–2013) — English writer, winner of Nobel Prize for Literature

Maya Lin (b. 1959) — American architectural designer and artist who designed the Vietnam Veterans Memorial in Washington, D.C.

Anne Morrow Lindbergh (1906–2001) — American writer and aviator

Alice Roosevelt Longworth (1884–1980) — American socialite, political wit, and eldest daughter of former U.S. President Theodore Roosevelt

Audre Lorde (1934–1992) — American writer and activist

Clare Boothe Luce (1903–1987) — American writer and diplomat

Mignon McLaughlin (1913–1983) — American journalist and writer

Nellie McClung (1873–1951) — Canadian politician and activist

Shirley MacLaine (b. 1934) — American actress, dancer, and writer

Sharon MacLatchie (b. 19??) — American writer

Madonna (b. 1958) — American singer/songwriter, actress, and activist

Wilma Pearl Mankiller (1945–2010) — Native American activist, first female Chief of the Cherokee Nation

Harriet Martineau (1802–1876) — English novelist, journalist, and economic and historical writer

Margaret Mead (1901–1978) — American cultural anthropologist and writer

Golda Meir (1898–1978) — Founder of the State of Israel and fourth Prime Minister of Israel

Angela Merkel (b. 1954) — German politician and the current Chancellor of Germany

Alice Meynell (1847–1922) — English writer and activist

Bette Midler (b. 1945) — American actress, singer/songwriter, and comedian

Margaret Millar (1915–1994) — American-Canadian writer

Marilyn Monroe (1926–1962) — American actress, model, and singer

Toni Morrison (b. 1931) — American novelist, editor, and professor

Alice Munro (b. 1931) — Canadian writer, winner of Nobel Prize for Literature

Iris Murdoch (1919–1999) — Irish-born English writer and philosopher

Martina Navratilova (b. 1956) — Czech-born American tennis player and coach

Florence Nightingale (1820–1910) — English nurse, founder of modern nursing, and social activist

Anaïs Nin (1903–1977) — French-born American writer

Kathleen Norris (b. 1947) — American poet and essayist

Flannery O'Connor (1925–1964) — American writer

Georgia O'Keeffe (1887–1986) — American painter

Jane O'Reilly (b. 1936?) — American writer and activist

Joyce Carol Oates (b. 1938) — American writer

Michelle Obama (b. 1964) — American lawyer, writer, and first African-American First Lady of the United States

Jacqueline Kennedy Onassis (1929–1994) — Former First Lady of the United States, activist, and editor

Gwyneth Paltrow (b. 1972) — American actress, singer, and writer

Emmeline Pankhurst (1858–1928) — English activist

Dorothy Parker (1893–1967) — American writer and poet

Rosa Parks (1913–2005) — American civil rights activist

Anna Pavlova (1881–1931) — Russian ballerina

Mary Pickford (1892–1979) — Canadian actress and film studio co-founder

Belva Plain (1915–2010) — American writer

Natalie Portman (b. 1981) — American actress

Anna Quindlen (b. 1952) — American writer, novelist, and journalist

Gilda Radner (1946–1989) — American comedian and actress

Jeanette Rankin (1880–1973) — American politician and first woman elected to Congress

Condoleezza Rice (b. 1954) — American diplomat, political scientist, and first African-American woman to serve as Secretary of State

Adrienne Rich (1929–2012) — American poet, essayist, and activist

Joan Rivers (b. 1933) — American comedian, writer, actress, and television personality

Eleanor Roosevelt (1884–1962) — American humanitarian, political activist, and longest-serving First Lady of the United States

J. K. Rowling (b. 1965) — English novelist

Helena Rubinstein (1870–1965) — Polish-born American entrepreneur

Sharon Salzberg (b. 1952) — American writer and teacher of Buddhism

Aung San Suu Kyi (b. 1945) — Burmese political leader

George Sand (1804–1876) — French writer

Sheryl Sandberg (b. 1969) — American business executive and writer

May Sarton (1912–1995) — American writer

Florida Scott-Maxwell (1883–1979) — American writer and psychologist

Diane Sawyer (b. 1945) — American broadcast journalist

Elizabeth Ann Seton (1774–1821) — First American saint

Gail Sheehy (b. 1937) — American writer, journalist, and lecturer

Florence Scovel Shinn (1871–1940) — American artist and writer

Margaret Chase Smith (1897–1995) — American politician

Patti Smith (b. 1946) — American poet and singer/songwriter

Susan Sontag (1933–2004) — American writer, filmmaker, professor, and political activist

Sonia Sotomayor (b. 1954) — U.S. Supreme Court Justice and first Hispanic to serve on the Court

Elizabeth Cady Stanton (1815–1902) — American social activist, abolitionist, and a pioneer of the women's rights movement

Gertrude Stein (1874–1946) — American avant-garde writer

Gloria Steinem (b. 1936) — American writer, journalist, and political and social activist

Elizabeth Stone (b. 19??) — American writer and professor

Sharon Stone (b. 1958) — American actress, producer, and former model

Harriet Beecher Stowe (1811–1896) — American writer and abolitionist

Meryl Streep (b. 1949) — American actress

Barbra Streisand (b. 1942) — American singer/songwriter, writer, actress, film producer, and director

Anne Sullivan (1866–1936) — American educator

Amy Tan (b. 1952) — American writer

Elizabeth Taylor (1932–2011) — British-born American actress and humanitarian

St. Teresa of Ávila (1515–1582) — Spanish mystic, Roman Catholic nun, and Roman Catholic saint

Mother Teresa (1910–1997) — Albanian-born Roman Catholic nun, declared Blessed in 2003, who devoted her life to the poor of Calcutta

Margaret Thatcher (1925–2013) — British politician and former Prime Minister of the United Kingdom

Marlo Thomas (b. 1937) — American actress, producer, and activist

Margaret Truman (1924–2008) — American singer, writer, and daughter of U.S. President Harry S. Truman

Sojourner Truth (1797–1883) — American abolitionist and activist

Harriet Tubman (1820–1913) — American abolitionist and humanitarian

Barbara Tuchman (1912–1989) — American writer and historian

Sophie Tucker (1884–1966) — Russian-born American singer, actress, and comedian

Tina Turner (b. 1939) — American singer and actress

Gloria Vanderbilt (b. 1924) — American artist, writer, heiress, and entrepreneur

Queen Victoria (1819–1901) — British monarch

Diane von Fürstenberg (b. 1946) — Belgium-born American designer

Harriet Van Horne (1920–1998) — American journalist and critic

Alice Walker (b. 1944) — American novelist, poet, and activist

Barbara Walters (b. 1931) — American broadcast journalist and writer

Martha Washington (1731–1802) — Former First Lady of the United States

Wendy Wasserstein (1950–2006) — American playwright

Faye Wattleton (b. 1943) — American educator and activist

Simone Weil (1909–1943) — French philosopher, Christian mystic, and activist

Mae West (1893–1980) — American actress, singer, screenwriter, and playwright

Ruth Westheimer (b. 1928) — German-born American sex therapist, writer, and media personality

Edith Wharton (1862–1937) — American novelist

Laura Ingalls Wilder (1867–1957) — American writer

Oprah Winfrey (b. 1954) — American media mogul, talk-show host, actress, and philanthropist

Debra Winger (b. 1955) — American actress

Naomi Wolf (b. 1962) — American writer and activist

Mary Wollstonecraft (1759–1797) — English writer, philosopher, and activist

Virginia Woolf (1882–1941) — English writer